Life'

Edited by Black Pear Press

With contributions by the entrants for the
Worcestershire Poet Laureate 2022-2023
Life's Wonders Anthology

This anthology is brought to you by
Rhianna Levi
and
Black Pear Press
in aid of Worcester Acute Hospitals Charity

WORCESTERSHIRE
ACUTE HOSPITALS
CHARITY
Putting patients first

Registered Charity Number. 1054612

Black Pear Press

Life's Wonders

First published in 2023
by Black Pear Press
www.blackpear.net

ISBN 978-1-913418-94-6

Cover image by Tony Judge & DALL·E 2
Cover design by Black Pear Press

Foreword

It has been an absolute pleasure to collaborate with Black Pear Press and Worcestershire Acute Hospitals Charity to make this remarkable anthology a reality. Since the beginning of my Worcestershire Poet Laureate tenure in June 2022, I have been working closely with the hospitals charity team to promote wellbeing, joy and belonging through written and spoken word.

I was inspired to focus this anthology on the theme of 'Life's Wonders' in response to the adversities that people have experienced, particularly in recent years. During times of struggle, human beings are outstanding in treasuring light within the dark, humanity during conflict, solidarity in times of sadness.

The world's beauty continues to make us gasp in awe, and it is a beauty that can be visible, subtle, or both. This anthology is a representation of numerous ways that life's wonders are observed. Furthermore, this anthology honours the diverse nature of Worcestershire Acute Hospitals NHS Trust, a remarkable community who treated my father, Stephen, with extraordinary care in his final months back in 2020.

For every copy sold of this anthology a donation will be made to Worcestershire Acute Hospitals Charity who in turn will invest it into Worcestershire Acute Hospitals NHS Trust. They will do this by providing enhancements, additions and added extras which link closely with the strategic aims of the Trust, that can make the working day easier, the service more comfortable or improve the experience for patients, staff and visitors.

A fitting tribute in alignment with the NHS turning 75 years old in 2023.

All my love
Rhianna Levi Worcestershire Poet Laureate 2022/23

Contents

Elder of Earth—Judith Sornberger

Inspired by the card in *The Gaian Tarot* by Joanna Powell
Colbert

Why do I pull you over and over, sitting alone
in your fading meadow, hair resting on your
shoulders like mine—still long as when we
were young and it gleamed chestnut in the
sunlight. Now it's the creamy white of the wool
you feed into the spindle of your spinning
wheel, the slight smile on your lips dreamy as
the early autumn afternoon where I ease into
the soft rhythm of the turning wheel. Like the
tapping circle of the jump rope I entered as a
girl, twirled by friends holding each end. Are
you, too, recalling those days as, one by one,
each scarlet apple drops from the tree behind
you? Even the doe grazing windfalls there—
eyes black needle pricks in the distance—
pauses to watch, to enter the spell of your
spinning. Because you wear a shawl of
bittersweet, I feel a colder season coming, wish
to pull its knitted warmth around me, to never
leave this moment, to never stop spinning one
thing into another.

Lemon Tree in the Algarve—Bex Hainsworth

In the corner of the villa's courtyard,
offering shade from late spring sizzle
to terracotta tiles, bare feet,
is a lemon tree.

There is a system of strange stars aching
amongst its branches. It is its own universe.

Hard moons softening in the sunlight,
the plumpest hanging low in the cupped
palms of broad leaves.

A flash of gold skin, covered with the same
dimples, pores, small grey bruises as bodies.
Living wrapping, yellow as currency.

One morning, after familiar sleeplessness,
my aunt chooses a star, brightest in its constellation.
With chipped nails and a triangular stone,
she cracks it open like a coconut.

A twist of white flesh and she is drinking;
pale, stinging juice runs down her wrists.

All through my uncle's illness, I have marvelled
at her ability to savour the world's sourest gifts.

The Five Stages of Grief—Brookly Taylor

The whole world stopped today.
Someone's loved one had died.
They marched in her absence
and sung instead of cried.
Darkness spread across the crowds,
everything had to be dreary and down.
Very little colour stood out on show,
apart from her coffin as she was
the most colour women ever known.

The whole world stopped today.
Just like mine did the day you died.
I remember the heart break
and the way I cried.
I just needed to say goodbye,
but you were already gone,
and life suddenly felt like a lie.

The whole world stopped today,
for our Queen.
She meant a lot to everyone,
just like you do to me.
The whole world stopped today.
I am still in disbelief.
Why didn't this happen when you left me?

Please—Heloise de Satge

Fill my cup with slippery sleep
and I will down it
in one, by which I mean I will take intermittent sips.

I want to sit
soft and live
hard. I will cushion
myself in the corner
of the room and rub
the small of your back until
it is whole, or at the very least until you are warm.

A Comparison to the Particulate—Colin James

When there is no one else about
we diners take our lunch outside
on the north side of the studio,
sit at a circular oak tree bench.
From here we can observe every possible approach,
even the top of the rail trail
leading down to the painted sea caves.
I often dine on local greens
drink hard water from a paper cup.
I could wander off if a garden maze
were near, lose myself despite familiarity
in the indelible confidence of acclimation.

Lay Me Down—Dee Dickens

Lay me down beneath a tree
when it is my time to sleep
perchance to dream a blanket of roots
wrapping me tighter, tighter, burn me,

lance my flesh,
divide what I no longer need,
distribute me that I may feed
older, younger, better, lesser.

I have no need for breathing
as the roots perforate;
I feel them, deep inside my lungs
crying, screaming defiantly.

A siren call to all of us
hold on, I'm coming, it gets better,
no more pain as my chest bursts wide open,
a flock of corvids taking flight.

My Guardian Angel—Ceinwen Haydon

She seems the same as ever, from a distance;
closer up, she's changed. One button missing.
another hanging by a thread. A loop of yarn
snagged, pulled loose. Her thick, blue cardigan
whiffs sour. Before, she always smelt so sweet;
her chosen scents, frankincense or lavender.
Her hair, once unruly curls, now droops limp
around her dry, creased cheeks. Her mouth
is crusted with porridge from a bland breakfast.
A lone, insistent follicle sprouts from her chin.
Her lilac, linen blouse sports smudged spots;
spills from drinks of coffee and tea. A dark patch
looks like blood, or tinned tomato soup. *Gran,
hello, how are you today?* She stirs from dozing,
focuses her milky eyes on me. Her candle smile
ignites from deep within her old body. *Sweetie,
so good to see you. Let's share a glass of sherry.*
We chatter on for hours, laugh hard, like always.

When I say goodbye, I realise, despite her lack
of dexterous fingers, her frailty and lived-in stains
my granny remains, very much alive with love.
All the rest is superficial, she's always been
my strongest ally. I know, in time, she'll watch
over me, chuckling, from her space in the skies.

Caring—Paul Smith

Could you be the one for me,
to live life's wonders wild and free?

I hope you do please understand,
to hold entwined each other's hands.

A kiss from you is all I seek,
to my heart's content that's not so bleak.

For your happiness that would be fine,
as long as you too could be mine.

Strolling along towards the path of light,
to be bonded to each other in a future bright.

Forever belonging to true love, we could be,
together forever, just you and me.

Autumn Morning—Robert John Perrin

The squirrels gambol in the trees
under a grey sky. The leaves
yellow, orange reds and greens.

Seeds are ripe, a welcome meal
for hungry kits outgrown mother's milk,
born last spring in a dray
in a bundle of warm twigs they lay.

As I look from my morning window
birds search for a meal.
Woodpigeons, magpies the occasional crow,
with this my fate is sealed.
Despite my problems it's good to be alive,
enjoying life, trying to survive.

Someone Noticed—Anna Emilia

In those times of uncertainty
dancing in the unknown,
battling with fate,
trying not to open the gate
but to collate with grace.

When someone sees
the tiny change,
the mini gleam,
how you exchanged your coffee for tea
because they know
that's your usual drink,
your usual routine.

You're beautiful,
you and your crucible.
The little things seem
like they are unseen
to the naked eye,
but only to those
with caring eyes.

Covid-19—Arun Kapur

We face a state of inhabitation,
more than ever, we face isolation.
The world rages in panic and they knock down
a virus spread in hysteria we drown.
Time of testing, a time to reveal true colour,
what is love without being true to the other?
A power brought to shine light on who is real,
those ready to fight, those ready to steal.
Join together more than ever,
Let us unite and find our treasure.

Little Acts of Love—Maya Jagger

Objects of love are transient.
I will never forget
the girl who got me sending heart emojis because I never
    used them.
The first guy I said "I love you" to.
The warmth I still feel from memories my friends left us; they
    left life before the rush.

I've felt less love this year
but when it's here
a soft intensity, it's worth the weight I feel in the heaviness
    of emptiness
from a place that expresses love unconditionally;

or from a song played by the DJ on their radio show,
or being acknowledged in the street
from a distance.
Little acts of love remain, people come and go

crossing boundaries
alive in our minds,
never leaving a trace,
at a slow and sexy pace.

If you're not feeling that right now,
it'll come back.

Verging on Beauty—Phil Knight

Shoots shatter cement.
Green buds bloom in
concrete cracks.
A riot of colour by
the tarmac treads.
Fantastic flowers
flood where traffic
flowed. Rewilding
and rewinding the
film of urban history.
Trees branches
break their boundaries.
Pollen replaces
pollution. Bees buzz
better than mechanical
motor mowers.
Absence, not
intervention, makes
all the difference.
Nature finds a way
when humanity is
lost in the deep dark
woods.

Fists—Stephen Paul Wren

Our fists side-by-side, palm-side down,
(four squares with turrets for knuckles),
remind me of our overlapping genes.
Your fists are perfect square,
adipose-smooth.
My fists are more imperfect,
scored with blue veins.
The similarity of our fists, though, is clear.
I want to see your DNA, learn its sequences,
immerse myself in its aqueous order.
So, I look at your fists.
So, that I can remember you
(the biological you)
on days when you are not physically here.
But, heavy cloud surrounds me, a delightful corpus.
There is so much more to you than fists.
Climbing out of your biology,
your nucleotides,
is your soul and, concurrently, your soul envelops your cells.
Your soul is beautiful,
gentle like Clementina.
Your fists don't throw punches,
they are only memorials to your existence here,
the merest heat
becoming parcels of love.
Our fists side-by-side, palm-side down,
our moment in time,
on Earth. Unearthing identity.

That Old Black Magic—S. A. Reeson

Grandad had *one* story,
his tale, of the morning
legend disappeared forever
legacy suppressed within
the Channel's December mists;
I never knew the truth.
Was he even stationed there?
RAF Twinwood Farm:
did he see Glenn,
did he speak to
Norman, or to John?
Perhaps, in retrospect
this again, a fabrication
bewitching childhood mind,
my skill, inherited in time;
five decades later,
still staring in wonderment,
was Miller's crossing
really made in 1944...?
Stories, lives that fade,
creation unmade
reanimates
between a subtle hiss,
remastered chronicle's
soft residue
magic, siren's song.

Citrus—Úna Nolan

I watch you peel clementines.
Strip the trailing wax skin
pull it clean in half and hold it to me.
I would eat from the flat of your hand,
juice stinging my eyes, and you can wipe
them clean, gently, under eyelids.
You touch every part of me I have left untouched,
I wear your citrus stained fingers
around my wrists, my shoulders, the small of my back;
my favourite piece of clothing,
keep me warm, hazy orange glow.

Favourite Little Things—Kevin Brooke

Little things, not enormous things,
are often the most wonderful things.

Memories of loved ones and mid-morning
rises, sunshine on Saturdays,
and clouds with disguises, of people,
pontoons, pepper pots and prizes
we'd won as surprises on days
that seemed lost.

Steps across stepping stones,
first signs of springtime,
releasing life's torment with
companions of a lifetime, compassion,
smiling and infinite coffeetime
from people who want nothing,
except your support

Lakeside reflections,
a stroll in the mountains, an arc
of a rainbow, the display of a fountain,
one slice too many, too much fun,
but who's counting, and Friday
night wine often drunk
just because.

Transporter—Rhianna Levi

Your bed became a lucid transporter
as the bells of 6am whistled with a morning brew and
   eagerness.

Your 6am looked slightly different,
as you gazed, drifting from an ageing body, below
into the freedom of air particles,
careless, with no reserve.

Your 6am was transported from one normality to another.
I think you are happier, more content now, with your new
   mornings.

The Person I am Today—Daniel Kay

The world is a cruel place
but it's also a beautiful place.
I'm disabled and I'm also alive.
I'm grateful for that and for the love and support of family
    and friends,
they help me through the tough times
and celebrate with me in the good times.
I'm grateful for the ability to see the world in a different way,
my disability gives me a unique perspective,
I wouldn't trade it for anything.
I'm grateful for the challenges disability has brought me,
it's made me a stronger and more resilient person.
I'm grateful for all the wonderful things about being disabled,
it's not always easy, but it's worth it.

I'm grateful for the strength I've found to keep going
when things are tough and I'm feeling low.
I'm grateful for the friends I've made along the way
who understand me and accept me for who I am.
I'm grateful for the obstacles I've overcome
that have made me the person I am.
I'm not always grateful for being disabled
but I'm learning to be,
because I know that it's not always easy.
But it's worth it.

Two Elephants in the Room—Keelan Carroll

Should we escape soon…just me and you?
I am tired of always standing in for unpleasant,
awkward things,
and I am sick to death of all these plastic friends
who make us feel like we don't belong with them.
But we could leave…just you and me.

We can trade this scene, and the apathetic feeling
that's within…for a sense of empathy.
Inky black skies and orange streetlights, an atmosphere
that'll be our ecstasy, tonight.

And in the morning, we can depart
or we could go back to mine, for an elephant
graveyard.

Wonderland—Dan Webber

Teenage boy applying lip-gloss in a supermarket mirror
'So he called me queer and I was like, yeah and?'
His friends giggle like it's no big deal
stealing from the samples. They trade eyeliners,
and ever so slightly
the world changes

Genre Fluid (Big White Shed, 2019)

something more grand than that—Linda M. Crate

i don't know how many
heartbreaks or deaths my heart has endured,
only that she has always risen from the
ashes on new flaming wings;

immortal phoenix
she does not know how to give up—

life is full of many wonders,
and i have so much i want to
experience and know even still;

i am so curious and eager to learn and grow—

don't really understand the people
who have already given up on themselves
or their dreams because i don't know how
to concede to defeat,

i am always hoping and dreaming and fighting;

because i refuse to settle for the mediocre
when i know i am meant for something
more grand than that.

Ask Twice—Phil Brennan

Me? I'm fine, mate,
of course I am,
I'm a bloke.

There's nothing wrong with me, pal,
nowt about me is broke.

I'm not sure why you're asking me.
Mither someone else instead.
I just keep myself to myself,
listening to the voices in my head.

If I choose to be a grumpy git,
or cry in a corner on my own,
it's just my way of dealing with things,
so please,
just leave me alone.

On second thoughts,
the fact you've asked,
I suppose it's really nice

so, next time I appear distracted,
it might be an idea to ask twice.

#AskTwice
#WorldMentalHealthDay2019

Patience—Lisa Millard

Patience, she whispers.
Revealing delicate whisps that span
across vast voids
engineered by the tiniest of creatures
crafted by moonlight.

Patience, she sighs.
Heart flies with the thrum of the buzzard
as he glides through the crack of dawn.

Patience, she groans.
Timber and bones
stretch and creak
in a decibel below silence.

Patience, she breathes.
Inconspicuous leaves expose themselves
almost translucent, with glowing veins
that provide highways for the welcome rains.

Patience, she hisses.
With each drop foundations relax
cages tremble and dissolve pushing
above the flood plain, eroding the bluff.

Patience, she exhales,
She inhales peace.

Now—Sanjeev Sethi

In orneriness
of laughter
your snaggleteeth
without a bumbershoot
like most of me.

Happiness:
a kerchief of kites
flying nowhere.

Chance of Rainbows—Erin Jamieson

The sky is pressed
with invisible rainbows
trapped underneath
grey, lugubrious clouds
that make my chest ache
with echoes of dreams
of lives I might have lived or
people I might have been but
I open the window for that sweet rush
of cool air and the clouds shift
just enough to catch a glimpse
of what's underneath.

Solar Swansong—Daniel Moreschi

When terra's tilt instils our skyward views,
the depths of lazuline begin to wear
a nascency of sudden subtle hues
that run as traces of a golden glare.

This fusion blurs and burns horizon lines
while pliant seas reflect a lasting haze:
a flight of fluid flames that intertwines
with clustered clouds until they're set ablaze.

A veil prevails, with flickering reach, yet leaks
a burgeoning, blackened blend it can't contain
that spreads a speckled shroud around the peaks
and trickles down akin to ashen rain.

A touch of twilight soothes the fervent zest
of reddened remnants duly laid to rest.

teeth marks—Lilly Ashton

when i see you chewing on a straw
i am sent back two years with a pop
the sudden ringing silence
as if it had been a gunshot
dark and hazy in a bar with a small dog
sitting near the entrance
up like a cannonball when the door opens
an aggressive little guardian

you are chewing on a straw
but the straw is my body
twisted into cylinder
pale and naked
teeth marks all over

(they say violence
is in the holding back)

New Reflections—D. I. Hughes

My mirror isn't glint with glass
nor does it hang on walls,
its telling all-time chime is you,
and you alone.

My mirror isn't stocked in shops
and clad with bargain tags,
yet rages bright in neon hues
to show me

that life is filled with prospect
if you stare back in signs,
echoing my actions,
holding to account,

how I react in kettle steam
but simmer when you look at me,
how I've curdled, head in hands,
new ways that glide on cooler sands.

My mirror isn't hung in Harrods
with fluorescent trims,
its living, breathing, mimicked teachings
is you.

All you.

To Hunger—Sarah Snyder

I embrace the word devour
not quite the way it enters

with surprising fuel at 5:00 o'clock,
a swelling ocean

of need—how good hummus tastes
with the crunch of pretzels or plantain chips.

No, more like when I head
outside into wind

with a desire for clouds,
for the bark of the dog

that lives down the street
or just the music of a dirt road

those pebbles and acorns.
O, the acorn, the woven

little wicker top, how intricate,
how full of perfect it is.

The Life of Eternity—Anna Green

It's only here, feeling so small
upon this rock, uneven and tall
that I know the value of my breath,
the precious moments between now and death.
I see so clearly that eternity exists
that these mountains, the rain, sun, and mist
have rested here upon this earth
for a dozen millennia before my birth.

Muse—Alshaad Kara

Why did my heart have to look beyond its own walls?

It got shot in your sight.
I was adamant to glue it back,
but there was no way to rekindle it.

My heart was glued to your heart,
it was adamant to make yours my heartbeat.
Do not coerce what it shall say!

Let my tears fall on your cheeks,
I got shot in your sight.
There was no way to rekindle that fascination again...

You are my breath,
an eternal heartbeat in heartbreak.

Secular and Sacred—Ade Couper

A forest: a grove made
of ancient oaks, yew, hawthorn,
ash, chestnut, beech:
these are the sacred places.
Sacred spaces
filled with spirit.
Places where those who wish to
can step away from the everyday;
immerse themselves in the sacred
and leave the secular—for a while.
Mighty oaks here replaces flying buttresses,
A Scots pine here serves
as a steeple:
but this is a mighty cathedral nonetheless,
truly one of life's wonders.
I come here to sit,
to meditate, to pray,
to simply be
and am refreshed,
renewed
purely from being here.

Ruminant—Linea Jantz

Time stops for no man

but it can pause

I breathe quiet on the shore

of a river frozen grey

autumn's stubborn leaves finally fall

pepper the melting snow

each step a softening

a gentle depression

beneath the arch of willows

the ducks float at the edges of the ice

I follow slight tracks of deer

into the forest

one perfect hoof print

a busy day's parenthesis.

Emily's Poem—Ian Henery

Six birthday candles
reflect
a child's smile
and laughing face
on this special day.

Linked together
with red thread,
our destiny.
You and I,
into eternity.

You are Chinese
and I
vegetarian,
Daughter and Father
sharing a bond
cascading into infinity.

Happy birthday,
little girl.
You are beautiful,
amazing
and I am so lucky
to be your dad.

I Imagine—Ellie Dart

I imagine
life birth and rip
itself from my skin.
It's ripe—pushes edges
to clutch the palms
of its mother. This
is something I may
not get to know.
But I see them
heave and breathe
before me tonight.

Shadow Selves—Leena Batchelor

We walk in shadows.
Our other selves loitering in the periphery holding our dreams
to account against the scales of conscience;
others of light held against the dark,
but even this we need to illuminate life's paths.

Voyeurs to dreams of man-made celluloid, beauty revered and
    fascination held,
too often destroyed in wanton ambition of greed and lust.
Wonders lost, but not eternally so.
Shadow's paragons walk among us.
The others of us.

They who deny the hold of constructed faith and rigid
discipline that keeps the freedom of belief at bay, deaf and
    sterile.
Among their wonders are sand castles in the sky, with dream
    dust illuminating their eyes.

Our other selves hold expectations, living dreams in reality's
present,
accepting cloud droplets falling on the sunset of final breaths,
able to imbibe dreams and peace,
where clouds of doubt hang suspended,
out of heartache's grasping reach.

Life is, always has been, always will be, a wonder.
Other selves embrace it,
Shadows yearn for its light.
Fear not the edges, peripheries of reality, shades of
    conscience—
without these, how would you know life's vibrant wonders?

Pact—Paul Case

The grass tickles our cheeks under
the sky yawning its blue oblivion.

'We've got so little time, don't we?'
you say.

I nod,
slide my fingers between yours
and hold on.

Musings from a Hospital Bed—Richard Banker

Some people like tiled front yards,
each groove and square speaks uniformity.
Some people like the call of the wild,
each sturdy oak and weeping willow lives for free
their branches hold out shelter and curtains.
I take the stately walk in the park
front doors shut by the onward creeping dark.
Some people like ready-made rules
it makes them feel that they belong.
Some people think that answers need more questions
as they seek the truth.
Some people have quite enough to do
to pay the bills, feed the kids, in daily toil
and living doesn't get any easier
except the night out on the town, momentary grace.
Some are not afraid to seek the muse
in poetry form, guitar shapes and paints
and fellow souls of different stripes and shapes
make us feel our community is made.
You don't see them on the tourist maps
the brown finger pointing sign in town
they won't win great riches or high renown.
If you have good sisters, fathers or true lovers
you can count yourself truly blessed
and all the ties that nurture, not bind
children, mothers, neighbours, friends and all the rest;
and not forgetting the resident artist
and not forgetting strong will and good health,
a compass to see you through these perilous days.

& a happy new year—Dorothy Lune

Time is loitering, directionless.
It wears a pink dress to settle in
arthritic cement, while its
lacklustre bus scoots to the next stop—
reverie: it's winter equinox at
Lake Erie, I wrapped my arm
around the frozen over lamp, its
gloomy face recognises me with its
illuminating arms of floe, which
are aimless & mean well. The
repercussive waves greet me at a
mild distance, they sigh like elders
who have melancholic bites. One
light allows a dress to be known,
the open corner store creaks for
attention / teenage cashier / fresh wine /
they sold fish & chips there so as
clever as I am I ate guarding the water.

When Choosing Flowers—Jaimes Lewis Moran

My mother has a strange approach, she chooses flowers based
     on names;
and the more eccentric these are, the better it seems!
Black lace elderberry alongside angel wings, and towering
     castor oil japonica's.

At the garden's front, there's a blue star and vivid bluebirds
     too.
Beside the gate was a smoke tree once, but I accidentally
     chopped it down!
My mother is the better gardener between us I will admit...

And now this flower choosing approach has found its way to
     me;
From golden feathers to butterfly gold,
Or french lavenders with hardy flowers so bold!

At one point I wanted a dracaena draco, the originally
     bleeding tree.
Or a redwood and coconut palm, even though I have no
     need for these.
Regardless, I still like the thought of what could've been...

When choosing flowers, what do you seek
In those garden centres all in bloom?
When finding new additions, what thoughts come to you?

Give Yourself a Break, You're the Only One who can—Alyssa Walker

Enjoy those golden moments
when you wake before the alarm,
wake, and don't return to slumber right away.

Enjoy the kisses you steal
from the one laid beside you
eyes crusted shut and lips a half-formed smile.

Enjoy the sun that creeps
through the sliver of a gap
left there on purpose, feel awash in the glow.

Reach one arm up, then two,
feel the snap crackle pop! of joints,
neglected bones, sprung to life once more.

Breathe the air of a new day
only slightly impeded by morning breath.
Smell the coffee brewed and waiting.

One last scratch behind the cat's ears
to the vaguely familiar songbird chorus—
I guess they're Zelda fans too.

The Importance of the Fly—Holly Gordon-Clark

Warblers wobbling out here,
airing myself in the duck's muffled cries;
the swing that gnaws my knees
that swiftly glides in the air.
My university is an echo, a figment of hair,
such a trivial fragment of undressing.

Undressing the sky as I feel my
bones raised in unity
or Ulysses.
You see
the confusion that I translate to you
on this page fights its way through
the ducks and little-birds-of-no-name.
The polluted air has such a song to it.

Skin that seeps through the holes of this reddish swing.
Murder is a crime only when the art is witnessed.

God, if my university option is the choice that defines life, is
life real at all?

The importance in that hollowing fly that hawks above me is
infinite.
Infinity in this world is nothing and this fly that droops and
hangs with a soft, distanced but undiscovered mind of its own,
its wings that my ogre-like eyes can hardly perceive glow.

As in the distance it floats away, hanging there for a second
with a most important glare. All of a sudden my perspective is
unveiled in the epiphany of the air.

Word-up—Natalie Peterson

I do not need any other blessing
but my own.
I was given what can't be stolen
it's all in my veins, with written words.
Conjuring up words to express how one feels
is already a blessing,
not everyone could express how they really feel
let alone start writing full verses.
I'm going to "blow my own trumpet"
because that's my personal present from the heavens
congratulating me on how I use it.
I know I've been fuelled with more poetic skills
regardless that I'm taking anti-psychotic tablets.
Yes, I'm taking it for granted
because if I wasn't granted it
what pastime would I have where I would be using my mental
strength?
I wouldn't want to start dabbling into something
knowing its outcome would be pointless.
I want to be able to plough
so then my gift has been manifested.
It's not all about being compensated
but my love for the present
and what you've accomplished with it.

Grasshopper in Calvados—Jan Hedger

What a dapper little chap he is,
in his jacket of copper veined,
enamelled exoskeleton of neon green,
like he'd jumped straight out from
a gentleman's outfitters, onto
the archipelago roadway, of heat
absorbing afternoon asphalt

and fixed himself there
for portraiture,
long back legs A Framed.

What a smug expression he has
a directness to his small bulbous
eyes, sweeping antenna's held in
perfect pivot balance. A superior
air of confidence, a boldness,
that piqued my curiosity to
to kneel down before him

and fix myself there
in understanding.
He knows who he is.

The Things We Barely Notice—Anthony Frobisher

The Things We Barely Notice

The passing of the sun,
the turning of the Earth,
the movement of time,
the rising and falling of tides.

The Things We Rarely Feel

The pulse of heartbeats,
the in and exhalation of breath,
the myriad daily thoughts,
the countless utterances of words.

The Things We Always Remember

The moments spent with loved ones,
the smiles and laughter of children,
the kindness of strangers,
the presence of friends.

The absence of you.

Blackberry Picking—Mike Wheeler

Sunny September afternoons
of childhood fondly remembered,
halcyon blue skies brushed
with cotton wool wisps of cloud.

The lanes near Halfpenny Green,
the buzz of small aeroplanes
overhead on Sundays, unhurried fall
of dandelion seed parachutes.

In a time of fewer cars standing
on the grass verge reaching
through bracken and cow parsley
to towering thorny brambles,

children's nettle-sting cries heard
nearby, looking for dock leaves
to soothe wounded knees exposed
in shorts and bare stung T-shirted arms.

And when the bags are filled
and the weight of them is ample
for a pie or two with bramleys
then home by car for Sunday roast.

A troop of liver purple-stained
hands and knees stand at the sink
and wash their stings, their grazed knees
and wait for Mother's call for lunch.

Wild Swim—Lorna Meehan

The sludge will try to suck me down.
My arms will tangle in those swaying tendrils.
But the sun is blazing a thousand diamonds,
and the still clear blue is begging me.
I am alone in the subtle crackles of nature's silence.
My body wants to be new again.
To float and be stroked by the world as it was
before limbs came along to move it.
I strip with a knowing grin,
feeling like of a siren of the loch,
and the swans can watch if they want to.
I welcome the cool caressing love the water gives me freely.
I breathe out and dip a tentative foot,
I'm going in.

A Glimmer of Hope—Mel Wardle Woodend

A shaft of sunlight
brings a glimmer of hope to
the darkest places.
A reminder that the sun
will rise each day regardless.

Breathless—Paige Taylor

Breathless,
those soft eyes sat with mine
and pulled their breath away
into stillness.
There is no word for that,
that moment which sits between
the breath in,
the breath out,
that stillness.
And yet there is where I sit
ever since those soft eyes sat with mine
I sit here in between the breath in
and the breath out.

Growth—Freddie Barker

I'm no longer eye-to-eye—or on the side

of my juvenile   misunderstanding   that:

for one to   leave the nest

they must take flight.

I once believed   that   to fly high,

one ought   to be   serene;

and brighter *and* lovely *and* clever enough

to charm the world   through a TV screen.

I left my mother's nest: only to hurtle

into the ground.

And from this rock-bottom, I could see how far I'd come.

Though   I yearned

to find solace in the soaring sky: instead

the sky   began to   rain.

and as my homesick malnutrition stripped my skin of

familiar pigments—I'd begun to bloom with new

colours.

Now unearthed; restored by the dirt;

within my grief I'd finally learned

one cannot grow their own roots without touching the ground

first.

Soulmates, plural—Eleni Brooks

I can't believe
that for so long
I thought I'd need
one man for this.
By this, I mean:
being told you
look beautiful,
unasked for cups
of tea, refilled
"I'm proud of you."
Bear hugs, high fives
into held hands,
being held at all,
needs for blankets,
chocolate, noticed,
a pyjamas kind of openness.
You do not need a husband
to be kissed on the head
just a friend
taller than you.

19th March—Muskaan Razdan

Spring in my bed drowned
the ocean under my back. I've spent
a season shedding skin and skins, in exile.
Today, the sun claimed its position. My feet drag,
in holey woollen socks, to hear it speak. Backyard
turns a bright shade of envy, as I leave. Church bells
harmonise with chirpings. Shadows crawl on buildings,
stretching for a better view. A crow is flying too close
to the ground. Take a breath for him. Find a bench
between the ribs of this gathering. Seat my coat
next to me. Let my left calf hang. Watch
saffron leak into the sky.
I resume.

Summer Skin—M. R. Smith

I feel the afternoon sun glaring at my bony shoulders, shaking
his head at my nakedness,

the sharp points of my bones, pushing hard through my skin,
like a flower turning their head for sunlight,

a soft prickling on skin that has been partially worn away by
the stronger rays of summer.

I'm reminded of the power the sun holds by the harsh tones
of red that have now appeared as the moonlight gently covers
my shoulder in a cool blue.

The wind whispers in the form of a soft breeze, kissing my
cheeks and burnt brows as I sip gently on cold water,

feet pushing into the dusty ground, black with the salt of the
earth, toes tinged with dry salt from dipping into rockpools as
we return home

my soles sore because they are not used to the pebbled
ground, but it is not enough to convince me that I should ever
wear shoes again.

Om Pomegranate (for Erica and Ella)—Ivor Daniel

Our baby overdue,
we drive to Ally Pally.

Perambulate damp dawn's
expectant movement.

Grey galleon London heaves
below, around.

Your tummy is a world. A globe.
A promise poem.

Our very own Om pomegranate.

On the next day
our daughter is born at home.
Miracle, meconium, more miracle,
and all manner of things are well.

And now, we have lived and loved
thirty years since then.

Tonight we watch TV—
it's Later with Jools Holland,
a special episode
with Arctic Monkeys live at Ally Pally.

In love with all these energies,
these mundane moments
and miracle affinities.

ClearView—Polly Stretton

193 steps,
Covent Garden tube,
waiting for a lift...
and there's a ClearView poster
asking *One Line or Two?*

It would have been wonderful
had there'd been ClearView
when we planned babies.
Imagine the waiting
endless waiting,
waiting for missing,
missing the month.
Two days late, three, four,
five, six?
Day seven—blood.

For sure, today
there's the same flood
of disappointment,
sadness
for a child who will never be.
A baby so real, that he or she
with a mop of dark hair
on a small, neat head
is more than a line on a ClearView test.

193 steps
Covent Garden tube,
waiting for a lift.

I've Seen Miracles—Wandering Biku

I've seen miracles happen before my eyes,
witnessed empty souls become human again.
More than human, I've seen them struggle
and fight against an invisible yet all-consuming, foe.
One who is dark, deceptive,
relentless and cruel.

I've watched them grow with a determination,
grace and humility unknown to the masses.
They have found new depths of consciousness
and understanding worthy of any monk or mystic.
Dark eyes once sunken now lifted and bright
and skin's pallor now blushed with hope.

And, yes, I've seen them fall and flounder
but never fail because once they have seen
how it can be, it doesn't leave them.
We may be pulled back under, time and again
by our demon of choice, but each time
we resurface with precious lessons learned.

Recovery is not just change, for change is too small a word.
It is not merely putting down the bottle,
ditching the pin or putting out smoke.
It's not just quitting. It's starting again.

It is renewed vitality, a different outlook,
a spiritual kick up the backside.
It can allow you to find what it was
you felt you were missing in life.
It is learning to let go whilst knowing
it's going to be OK.

Motherland—Liv Gamble

I'm no patriot,
not in the way you'd recognise.
I don't love the red, white, or blue.
It's the green I'm promised to,
the crown of every hill
and the tail of every valley,
the land alive with every swell and adagio
playing for the eyes—
and what a singer Mother is.
Lullabies hummed in the sleep of winter,
every thunderstorm an orchestra,
the hiss of her song behind the rain.
We listen with awe,
her babes in the woods,
each little village nestled in the divots
of her cupped palms,
hamlets pressed against her chest,
all of us children in the arms of the Mother.
We are buoyed and fed
as new-borns,
our mouths forever suckling on the teat.
Doubtless there'll be another
quite like her,
every flower a brain,
every river a vein
running to the ocean heart,
beating, as it does,
with every pull and push of the tidal blood.
I'm no patriot,
but I am family here, in kin and in love—
forever a child to the wide, open Motherland.

Wonder Girl—Carol Fenwick

Torchbearer of liberty, light shining on your face.
Your name means God is gracious, or alternatively, peace.

I am touched by your kindness, life giving warm light.
When you left someone switched on the darkness of night.

It feels cold without you. No more warmth from your smile.
You continue with grace, where you work and reside.

I never forget what we had and what is left.
I am struggling inside and somewhat bereft.

The spirit lives long and offers so much.
We touched each other's lives and God loves us so much.

Whatever life holds, between future and past,
there will be special moments to cherish and last.

When you look at my keyring gift, do you think about what we
    discussed?
Believe in ourselves, that is what we must trust.

Beauty of Words—Andy N

I wonder if nature knows how beautiful it is
when the flowers begin to stretch awake,
as winter finally sinks into the dawn of spring
like the very essence of life itself,
when we recently held my wife's nephew in our arms
watching the puzzlement in his face for hours.

I wonder if the world knows how it inspires us every day
whether it is sunshine or rain or something in between,
from inside our homes or on the road to somewhere else,
curling everything we think into a series of miracles
strung across the morning air in the middle of a forest
patterning words in a relief full of life.

The Return—Javi Cain

Walking again on the worn path
to the beach, the sand comes through soft
underfoot. Mild hills rise and descend
in a tender sway, as if breathing,
while grasses dry rustle in the wind
each stalk touching among a murmured crowd.
And beyond the crested hill, the sea moves restlessly,
rumbling in a tumbled thrall, an unsettled
god, fingering over and over
the edges of this bewildering world.

Her Name is Nature—Beth Wood

An open window in a thunderstorm
just to hear the small kisses of the rain.
None can describe the peace that is born
from the slivers of silver to my brain.
I have sat, a statue, and watched for hours,
on the damp windowsill, hand outstretched,
feet curled around my forgotten flowers,
into my stricken soul this became etched.
The power of this earth has been lost,
but here I see her claim it back in force.
We should listen as she should not be crossed
for this power is known to run her course.
And although she never outwitted death,
something forever takes its first breath.

Nature's Rebirth—Linda Downs

She was a tree branch,
living art formed
from her mother's trunk,
roots of her ancestors
breathing life into purpose.
He called himself a sculptor
so, she let him strip her bark,
reshape and trim her rough edges,
a human only defined by beauty.
And when they came to fawn
her eyes were open
to the Frankenstein creation
and the forest that she left
called to her in dreams.
You set alight to her crown
with a fire cap of blinding rage
and when the smoke cleared
she rose again from ash.

Beyond the Pane—Des Mannay

The view has become full of promise,
as nesting birds in pairs
signify a change of luck.
And flowers, as if in a relay race,
pass the baton from one species to another.
Crocuses and snowdrops to daffodils,
daffodils to bluebells and tulips.
Earthworms and roots below are furiously
burrowing, the surface appears a place
of peace, swans on a lake. This germination
is like imagination—here seeds, like ideas grow,
challenging the 'Old Season'—which has had its day.
Just as the blossom on the trees give way to fruit
and berries of the black, the green and red—
which become a store of energy
in the struggle for longer days,
as we strive to keep darkness at bay,
there will be time enough for darkness
in the winter of our lives.

Having Another Convincing Conversation—
Nigel Astell

Lips moving one-way direction
my imagination joins another:
Who's that sitting there?
That's my invisible friend.
Don't be daft, Grandad
What are you talking about?
He owns an invisible bike
I could borrow it
when going to Mc Donald's.
He says you can
jump on the back.
Don't be daft, Grandad.
Two happy meals eaten
time to go home,
tugging my arm hard:
Please let's go back
Why what is wrong?
Do we have to?
Is it Mr Teddy?
Is it your coat?
Is the free toy?
No, No, No, No,
we must go back
for your friend's bike.

Constellation—Dangermouse#

I'm a constellation,
a collection of stars,
off, somewhere you can't reach,
all yellow and sharp edges.

From afar, I twinkle the same as things close to home,
by stream or grass blades, through dream
catchers and lamp shades,
dancing lights, skating the glint in your eye.
All yellow and sharp edges.

A reflection.
morning its former self
somewhere you can't reach
in the pitch black, with a sprinkle of salt;
the explosions long over before you see the
results.
All yellow and sharp edges.

From afar, I glitter the same way dreams do.
A closed eye, a single tear, a clenched promise
and a handful of fear.
All yellow and sharp edges.

Someone's lying, are we falling or flying?
Somewhere you can't reach.
A shooting star.
All yellow and sharp edges.

Orb around My Bed—Sarer Scotthorne

Thursday has no poem,
it has a door to close.
Cotton from Egypt to hide
myself against the soft outside upheaval.
The deepest darkest night river
has stars swallowing,
moment by moment, my attention.
Consciousness is fundamental to every cell,
potential—unknown unrecognisable.

I have a door to close,
cotton from Egypt.
There are plainly ethical dilemmas,
about my luxury—I know. I see,
but here, more grey seals.
Despite our
night seas forced swallowing
rewilding the night sky
the challenge is our
taken-for-granted intuitions.

Release the beavers to reshape—
imagined neural pathways.
There is spiritual energy to focus on.
Time, on seconds, time-on moments.

Geography Inside a Volvo—Jone Rush MacCulloch

Drive past the dry, dusty arroyo
on a dirt road, a chorus of crickets.
The sweet pungency of fescue
a first kiss, wet and sloppy.
Past curfew, novice cartographers
discover parallel longitudes.
Breath fogs the windows
our lips, body compasses.
Turn right at the mole behind your ear
and trace the scar above my eye.
Find the mouth a second time
our hands mapping new routes.

—Brief Life Cycle of a Fruit Fly—Zoe Dempsey

—shell,
      dewdrop,
            moonshine. Wrapped in rotting.
Larva. Stir awake. I am moondrop!

      the
         fall

—dig! Pry away the blue. Under almond skin, I pupate.
Breathe, growing pains,   almond light—

I am,
winged soul.
The scent of death,
I sing, mouth water.
Find the rot.
      Sugar! Feast. Others!
      My little soul!

            torn to little souls. So soon,
         I am mother.   No hunger—